Just the Right Word

Just the Right Word

Gilbert H. Caldwell

ABINGDON PRESS
NASHVILLE

JUST THE RIGHT WORD

Copyright © 1996 by Abingdon Press

This book is printed on recycled, acid-free elemental-chlorine–free paper.

ISBN 0-687-017262

96 97 98 99 00 01 02 03 04 05 — 10 9 8 7 6 5 4 3 2 1

MANUFACTURED IN THE UNITED STATES OF AMERICA

These words are dedicated to my parents who taught me and my sisters to "march to the beat of our own drummers."

To my wife, Grace, who personifies in spirit and practice the meaning of her name. To my son Dale Gilbert Caldwell, the Management Consultant, who runs marathons and who has made of his life a "race" to bridge the gaps between human need and opportunity. To my son Paul Douglass Caldwell, the Engineer, who has maintained his capacity to be an artist in performance and personality.

To the churches it has been my privilege to pastor, to the church-related institutions where I have worked,

and,

to the friends who have been there when I needed them, or who sometimes could not be there,

All of you have been important to me. Thank you.

The words and thoughts in this book are for you, for us, and for those whom we will never know.

> Gilbert Haven Caldwell
> St. Mark's United Methodist Church,
> in the Village of Harlem
> in the City of New York

Introduction

*All of us have favorite scriptures,
quotations, stories, and so on, that we
remember and turn to at different
moments in our lives. My family often
reminds me that I have the capacity to tell
the same story over and over. My mother used to say that in
her family, when someone was repeating an oft-heard story,
some family member would call attention to the fact by
saying, "Ten fingers and ten toes." As my mother got older,
she would repeat over and over again the same stories and
quotations. However, none of us dared to say to her, "Ten
fingers and ten toes!"*

I offer the following quotations with love and affection. I hope they will strike such a chord with you that
you will begin to use them often.

Contents

As We Are

M ost of the evil is not done by evil people, but rather by good people who do not know that they are not good.

REINHOLD NIEBUHR

Do not be overcome by evil, but overcome evil with good.

ROMANS 12:21

It is difficult to accept and acknowledge the fact that we are not as good as we pretend, or want to be. We live our lives in comparison to others, and when we compare ourselves to some people, we look pretty good. However, we are learning that great damage may be done to our spirits if we live in denial, when we persist in avoiding seeing ourselves as we really are.

May we experience the liberation that comes when we are honest with ourselves and about ourselves. The place to start is to compare ourselves to Jesus rather than to any other person. Surely we will fall short in the comparison, but if we remember that God never stops loving us, no matter what, we can continue to strive to live as Jesus lived. We may never be as good as we *wish* to be, but by acknowledging our weakness and accepting God's help, we can be better than we are.

Almighty and most merciful God, who has given us a new commandment that we should love one another, give us also grace to fulfill it. Make us gentle, courteous, and forbearing. Direct our lives so that we may look to the good of others in word and deed. Hallow all our friendships by the blessing of thy Spirit, for the sake of your Son, Jesus Christ our Lord.

BROOKE FOSS WESTCOTT

Judgment

very time you point one finger at someone, you are pointing three at yourself!

AN OLD PROVERB

Do not judge, so that you may not be judged.

MATTHEW 7:1

inger pointing is something that all of us do. We are confident that we are astute and aware enough to determine when someone is at fault. There is almost an eagerness in identifying an individual's flaws. Yet we are told that human beings engage in something called "projection." We project onto others some of the flaws that we know we possess.

When we become aware of our own imperfections, we become instantly more tolerant and patient of the flaws we see in others. Jesus urged us not to judge others. Furthermore, he warned that "with the judgment you make you will be judged, and the measure you give will be the measure you get" (Matthew 7:1-2). The next time you find yourself becoming angry at another's imperfections, look inside yourself; what "log" is in your own eye?

Grant, O God, that we may keep a constant guard upon our thoughts and passions, that they may never lead us into sin, that we may live in perfect charity with all [others], in affection to those who love us, and in forgiveness to those, if any there are, that hate us. Give us good and virtuous friends. In the name of our blessed Lord and Savior Jesus Christ.

WARREN HASTINGS

The Shepherd

I know the psalm, but he knows the shepherd.

ANONYMOUS

Surely goodness and mercy shall follow me all the days of my life: and I will dwell in the house of the LORD for ever.

PSALM 23:6 KJV

It is easy to substitute our ability to "talk the talk" for our inability to "walk the walk." We who profess faith can sometimes mouth words that we have not internalized. A simple way to say this is to say that we often do not practice what we preach.

Life in the church sometimes produces persons who have never bought what they are attempting to sell. Faith that is a word, without deed, is less than faith.

But before we begin to list the persons we know who fit this description, honesty compels us to say that we, too, live with a vast gap between our professed belief and our practice of our belief.

The answer to our dividedness is to get to know and accept the Shepherd, and to stay in constant communication with him.

O God, our true life, to know you is life, to serve you is freedom, to enjoy you is a kingdom, to praise you is the joy and happiness of the soul. I praise and bless and adore you. I worship you, I glorify you. I give thanks to you for your great glory. I humbly beg you to live with me, to reign in me, to make this heart of mine a holy temple, a fit habitation for your divine majesty.

ST. AUGUSTINE

Rejoice in Hope

od has made us that we can somehow bear pain and sorrow and even tragedy.

GEORGE E. WESTBERG

Rejoice in hope, be patient in suffering, persevere in prayer. Contribute to the needs of the saints; extend hospitality to strangers.

ROMANS 12:12-13

None of us relishes pain, sorrow, or tragedy. We live in hope that somehow we might avoid the devastating and debilitating impact of this trinity of disruption. When we cannot avoid their awful reality, we often cry aloud, "Why me, God? Why me?"

Yet many of us can testify that we have been able to survive and endure those experiences that transform our relatively smooth life's journey into moments of rocky and rough travel. We have been able to survive because the God of our creation has equipped us to live with, live in spite of, those experiences that throw us off balance.

God enables us not only to bear, but also to transform what we experience as negatives into a grief process that can be healing. Therefore, we no longer fear the inevitable coming into our lives of pain, sorrow, or even tragedy, because the God who equips is always present to point us toward the future.

If thou meet with the cross on thy journey, in what manner so ever it be, be not daunted, and say, Alas, what shall I do now? But rather take courage, knowing that by the cross is the way to the Kingdom.

JOHN BUNYAN

Real Strength

Nothing is as strong as gentleness; nothing is as gentle as real strength.

ATTRIBUTED TO THE NATIVE AMERICAN COMMUNITY

Let love be genuine; hate what is evil, hold fast to what is good; love one another with mutual affection; outdo one another in showing honor. Do not lag in zeal, be ardent in spirit, serve the Lord.

ROMANS 12:9-11

*O*ften people become confused about what it means to be strong. We grow up believing that strength is related to the capacity to push, pull, jerk, and suppress others.

Leaders are especially at risk in believing that one's effectiveness is determined by the ability to limit and control those with whom they work and play and plan.

We are so afraid of appearing weak or vulnerable that we flex our muscles at every opportunity. Yet, in our heart of hearts, we know we are pretending strength as a way to cover weakness.

Let us not be afraid to be gentle and sensitive and kind and attentive and flexible. We have a model in Jesus. Let us imitate him.

O Christ our God, who are yourself the fulfillment of the law and the prophets, and did fulfill all the ordered purpose of the Father, always fill our hearts with joy and gladness, now and for ever, world without end.

LITURGY OF ST. CHRYSOSTOM

Struggle

here are some persons who want rain without the thunder and lightning. They want crops without plowing up the land. But if there is no struggle, there is no progress.

FREDERICK DOUGLASS

"At an acceptable time I have listened to you, and on a day of salvation I have helped you."

2 CORINTHIANS 6:2

*M*ost of us would rather avoid struggle. We view struggle as debilitating, depressing, and sometimes disgusting. We want life without the stresses and strains, but we must admit that we have been shaped for the better by some of our struggles. Perhaps it is time we began to view struggle in more positive ways because of the way it molds and shapes us for the better.

Certainly, none of us wants to go out looking for struggle, but when difficulties come we can be reassured by the words of Martin Luther:

A mighty fortress is our God,
A bulwark never failing;
Our helper he amid the flood
Of mortal ills prevailing.

A "Standing Up" Spirit

he toy bounces back up, no matter how hard I hit it, because he's standing up on the inside.

A CHILD'S COMMENT ABOUT A
CHRISTMAS TOY

Now the Lord is the Spirit, and where the Spirit of the Lord is, there is freedom.

2 CORINTHIANS 3:17

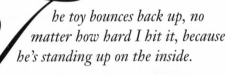

*I*f we live long enough, something within us or something outside us will knock us down spiritually, psychologically, or physically. Unfortunately, none of us can avoid the "knockdowns" of life. Paul, whose letters appear in the New Testament, said at one point, "Although I have been knocked down, I have not been knocked out."

The child's understanding of why the toy bounces back up applies to us. We cannot avoid being knocked down, but a "standing up" spirit within enables us to come back, and come back again. Hallelujah! Hallelujah!

Let nothing disturb you,
nothing alarm you: while
all things fade away
God is unchanging. Be patient
and you will gain everything:
For with God in your heart
nothing is lacking,
God meets your every need.

TERESA OF AVILA

Ready or Not

 *eady or not, here I come!*

FROM THE GAME HIDE-AND-SEEK

Although he was a Son, he learned obedience through what he suffered; and having been made perfect, he became the source of eternal salvation for all who obey him.

HEBREWS 5:8-9

The person who is designated "It" in hide-and-seek shouts these words before he or she begins looking for those who are hiding.

Perhaps God had similar thoughts as God decided to send the One whom we know as Jesus into human history. God the Creator and All-knowing One knows our frailty and fragility. God knew we would never be "ready" to receive Jesus. Nevertheless, a caring and concerned God dared to share in human form a portion of the Divine Self.

It is because God understands our unreadiness that we are able to say *yes!* to the greatest gift of all, Jesus, who is Comforter, Liberator, Savior, and Redeemer.

Jesus, the very thought of thee
With sweetness fills the breast;
But sweeter far thy face to see,
And in thy presence rest.

BERNARD OF CLAIRVAUX

Reconciliation

All this is from God, who reconciled us to himself through Christ, and has given us the ministry of reconciliation; that is, in Christ God was reconciling the world to himself, not counting their trespasses against them, and entrusting the message of reconciliation to us. So we are ambassadors for Christ, since God is making his appeal through us; we entreat you on behalf of Christ, be reconciled to God.

2 CORINTHIANS 5:18-20

*R*econciliation is moving from division to togetherness, from brokenness to wholeness, from resistance to acceptance. Recall the wonderful feelings you have had when you have made up with someone with whom you have had a disagreement. Yet pride, hurt, misunderstanding, and fear often keep us from the joy of reconciliation.

It is, therefore, important to understand that in Jesus we have an example, a model, a mentor to guide us in becoming reconciled with those with whom we have been at odds.

The world, nation, community, church, and family need to see over and over again the miracle that is possible, called reconciliation.

> *But drops of grief can ne'er repay*
> *The debt of love I owe;*
> *Here, Lord, I give myself away;*
> *'Tis all that I can do.*

> ISAAC WATTS

Trust

rust, or the lack of it, is at the root of success or failure in relationships and in the bottom-line results of business, industry, education, and government.

STEPHEN R. COVEY

And we want each one of you to show the same diligence so as to realize the full assurance of hope to the very end, so that you may not become sluggish, but imitators of those who through faith and patience inherit the promises.

HEBREWS 6:11-12

*T*here is in these competitive and sometimes frightening and fearful times a reluctance to believe that persons with whom we work and worship and even play are worthy of our trust. We have grown to assume that a cautious or even suspicious response to others is necessary for our survival. We even describe these responses as being healthy.

Yet, to live our lives unable to trust keeps us from experiencing the rewards of trusting. We miss out on some of the joy, some of the bonding, some of the mysterious magic that is produced when two or more persons experience each other with openness and candor. Our inability to trust must push us to ask ourselves, "Am I worthy of being trusted by others? What am I saying about myself in the ways that I respond to those around me?"

*Be gracious to all that are near and dear to me
and keep us all in thy fear and love. Guide us,
good Lord, and govern us by the same Spirit,
that we may be united to thee here as not to be
divided when you are pleased to call us hence, but
may together enter into thy glory, through Jesus
Christ, our blessed Lord and Savior.*

JOHN WESLEY

Transformation

I f you always do what you always did, you will always get what you always got.

JACKIE "MOMS" MABLEY

But God proves his love for us in that while we still were sinners Christ died for us. Much more surely then, now that we have been justified by his blood, will we be saved through him from the wrath of God.

ROMANS 5:8-9

The late comedian Jackie "Moms" Mabley delighted many of us with her humor. She's right. If we persist in doing what we have always done, then there is little chance that the results achieved will be different from what they have always been. This is why we seek transformation with all of its many manifestations. Life takes on new degrees of excitement when we dare to change and create and do things differently.

Christ died that we might live. His blood, given for us, is the power we need for transformation.

This is all my hope and peace:
Nothing but the blood of Jesus.
This is all my righteousness:
Nothing but the blood of Jesus.

ROBERT LOWRY

Duty

I have tried to be a dutiful presbyter, although I have little relish for still more committee work and no taste for church politics.

DAVID H. C. READ

So it depends not on human will or exertion, but on God who shows mercy.

ROMANS 9:16

avid H. C. Read, former pastor of Madison Avenue Presbyterian Church in New York City, speaks for all of us who have attempted to be "dutiful," even when we felt we could not keep our sanity if we attended one more church meeting. It is amazing what love of, and belief in, the church in its denominational forms makes us do. We participate in the politics, we attend meetings, even when we wonder if God is in our machinations in meetings.

One of the more amazing attributes of God is that God helps make sense of much of our organizational nonsense. Hallelujah!

Most merciful Father, we confess that we have done little to forward your kingdom and advance your glory. Pardon our shortcomings and give us greater zeal for your service. Make us more ready and diligent by our prayers, by our alms and by our examples, to spread the knowledge of your truth and to enlarge the boundaries of your Kingdom; and may we do it all to your glory.

WILLIAM WALSH HOW

Aging

*T**he salient fact is obvious
enough: "old" people are people
who have lived a certain number of
years, and that is all.***

ALEX COMFORT

*The righteous flourish like the palm tree,
     and grow like a cedar in Lebanon.
In old age they still produce fruit.*

PSALM 92:12, 14*a*

Most of us want to live a long time, but we do not want to get old. "Oldness" carries a stigma, a negative quality. Stereotyping is not limited to persons because of race, gender, or place of origin. We stereotype the aging without realizing we are stereotyping. Still, we want to live long enough to be old. Let us not dismiss, minimize, marginalize those who have lived for many years. Rather, let us live in joyful anticipation of our becoming old.

As we grow older, God's purpose for our lives may become clearer. Things that worried us when we were younger no longer hold the threat they once did. Aging may bring us an inner peace, so that we can say with Brother Lawrence:

I know not what God purposes with me, or keeps me for; I am in a calm so great that I fear naught. What can I fear, when I am with Him? May all things praise Him.

Gifts

ere we [persons of African descent] have brought our three gifts and mingled them with yours: A gift of story and song . . . a gift of sweat and brawn . . . a gift of the spirit.

W. E. B. DUBOIS

In every nation anyone who fears him and does what is right is acceptable to him.

ACTS 10:35

*E*ach person, each group of persons by virtue of their heritage, history, culture, and experience brings to all of us the particular gifts that are theirs. We all are richer because we have stood and lived in the presence of those who are different from ourselves. A human tragedy is that some persons have not claimed their gifts and others have been unable or unwilling to receive the gifts of others.

It is impossible to live this life and not be touched and shaped by those whose journey has been different from our own. We rejoice as we acknowledge those differences.

In him shall true hearts everywhere
Their high communion find;
His service is the golden cord
Close binding humankind.

JOHN OXENHAM

Grace

f we must die, O let us nobly die,
So that our precious blood may not be shed
In vain; that even the monsters we defy
Shall be constrained to honor us though dead!

CLAUDE McKAY

"And you will know the truth, and the truth will make you free."

JOHN 8:32

*T*he experience of oppression ignites a spirit of resistance among the oppressed that is rooted in our need as humans to be free from the artificial restrictions imposed upon us by others. History has shown us that hate produces hate, violence produces violence. Today let us strive to create a society that so values the human spirit that violent death loses its nobility.

Let us pray that grace may everywhere abound
And a Christ-like spirit everywhere be found.

CHARLES H. GABRIEL

Praying for Our Enemies

*L*ord Jesus Christ who hast commanded us not to return evil for evil, but to pray for those who hate us, enable us by thy blessed example and thy loving spirit, to offer a true prayer for all our enemies (and especially for those persons known to Thee, who have wrought us harm).

PRAYER FOR OUR ENEMIES

"Those who were not my people
I will call 'my people,'
and her who was not beloved I
will called 'beloved.'
"And in the very place where it
was said to them, 'You are
not my people,'
there they shall be called
children of the living God."

ROMANS 9:25-26

*O*ne of the greatest challenges for those of us who are on a spiritual journey is the challenge to our spirits by those who seem to dislike or even hate us. We are tempted to respond to them in ways similar to the ways they treat us. Yet, we know this is not the way to nurture our spirits, or to be helpful to them.

The words from the Prayer for Our Enemies, published more than fifty years ago, is a reminder that those persons who disturb us belong on our prayer lists. They, more than any others, challenge us to "let go and let God."

When you are tempted to return bitterness with bitterness, stop and remember—that person is one for whom Christ died.

Wait, my soul, upon the Lord,
To his gracious promise flee,
Laying hold upon his word,
As thy days, thy strength shall be.

WILLIAM F. LLOYD

Remembrance

We here highly resolve that these dead shall not have died in vain; that this nation, under God, shall have a new birth of freedom; and that government of the people, by the people, for the people, shall not perish from the earth.

ABRAHAM LINCOLN
THE GETTYSBURG ADDRESS

For whatever is born of God conquers the world. And this is the victory that conquers the world, our faith. Who is it that conquers the world but the one who believes that Jesus is the Son of God?

1 JOHN 5:4-5

*D*etermining the legacy that we want to preserve in response to those who have died is a major responsibility for individuals, families, and a nation. Abraham Lincoln, in his Gettysburg Address was clear about how those killed at Gettysburg and in other battles of the Civil War should be remembered. We are challenged each day to make sure that those who have died for those of us who still live are remembered. We remember them best by incorporating into our lives the principles, practices, and philosophies that reflect the quality of their life and death.

Faith of our fathers! we will love
Both friend and foe in all our strife;
And preach thee, too, as love knows how
By kindly words and virtuous life.

FREDERICK W. FABER

Oneness in Christ

*W*e shall be alike—brothers of one father and one mother, with one sky above us and one country around us, and one government for all. Then the Great Spirit Chief who rules above will smile upon this land, and send rain to wash out the bloody spots made by brothers' hands from the face of the earth.

CHIEF JOSEPH

For just as the body is one and has many members, and all the members of the body, though many, are one body, so it is with Christ.

1 CORINTHIANS 12:12

hief Joseph of the Nez Perce tribe reminds us of our oneness in creation. Brothers against brothers, rather than brothers and sisters in solidarity with each other, is one of the negative mysteries of our human journey. We who spring from the same Source find it difficult to live with one another. Our disagreements become debates and our debates too often become conflicts and those conflicts can become violent. We then inflict tragic pain upon one another. Worst of all, the conflicts of former generations are often lived out by successor generations.

Our human history, our present, and our future, are so intertwined that we must find ways to celebrate our common bloodlines, rather than engaging in conflict that sheds our blood.

We share each other's woes,
Our mutual burdens bear,
And often for each other flows
The sympathizing tear.

JOHN FAWCETT

Their Story Is Our Story

For my people thronging 47th Street in Chicago and Lenox Avenue in New York and Rampart Street in New Orleans, lost, disinherited, dispossesed . . .

MARGARET WALKER

As servants of God we have commended ourselves in every way: through great endurance, in afflictions, hardships, calamities, beatings, imprisonments, riots, labors, sleepless nights, hunger; by purity, knowledge, patience, kindness, holiness of spirit, genuine love, truthful speech, and the power of God; with the weapons of righteousness for the right hand and for the left; in honor and dishonor, in ill repute and good repute.

2 CORINTHIANS 6:4-9

Margaret Walker, the daughter of a Methodist minister, captures in her poem "For My People" the rhythms, moods, joys, and struggles of a people who with amazing patience survived, and in some places even thrived, against overwhelming odds. The stories and pilgrimages of one people are shared by all people. Each family and group has its own stories of struggle, suffering, triumph, and more struggle. Therefore, we cannot afford to be indifferent or distance ourselves from the biographies of any people. Their story is our story.

Not alone we conquer, not alone we fall;
  In each loss or triumph lose or triumph all.
Bound by God's far purpose in one living whole,
Move we on together to the shining goal.

FREDERICK LUCIAN HOSMER

As a Mother

One of the best-kept secrets of the church is the fact that the Bible itself sometimes describes God in feminine terms. By recognizing the image of the female in God, the ancient Hebrews also affirmed that the female is made in God's image.

SHARON NEUFER EMSWILER

*As a mother comforts her child,
so I will comfort you;
you shall be comforted in
Jerusalem.*

ISAIAH 66:13

*D*o you ever wonder, as I do, what Creator God must think about our responses to Creation? The magnificent evidence of Divine creative activity is seen in persons, in the environment, in space; yet we collide with one another in our efforts to define, limit, and even exclude some elements of Creation. A careful and sensitive reading of the Bible identifies and lifts up the inclusivity of Creation. May we experience the joyful excitement that comes from affirmation rather than negation and denial. Life is too short, Creation is too wonderful, to do anything else.

O LORD, my heart is not lifted
 up,
  my eyes are not raised too
   high;
I do not occupy myself with
  things
  too great and too marvelous
   for me.
But I have calmed and quieted
  my soul,
  like a weaned child with its
   mother;
  my soul is like the weaned
   child that is with me.

PSALM 131:1-2

Those People

I feel that the outer poverty, injustice, and absurdity we see when we look around us mirror our own inner poverty, injustice, and absurdity. The poor man or woman outside is an invitation to the poor man or woman inside.

Whoever gives even a cup of cold water to one of these little ones in the name of a disciple—truly I tell you, none of these will lose their reward.

MATTHEW 10:42

We label some people because of their predicament, their social circumstance, "those people." We see them, but we do not want to see them. We have devised ways to make them invisible because their very existence disturbs us. But there is something about God's created order that binds us as humans to one another. We are family, whether we wish it or not. Therefore the plight of others awakens in us our own inner plight. We cannot separate and distance ourselves from others because of their circumstances. Rather our spiritual journeys cause us to connect their external plight that we see and are disturbed by, to our inner plight that neither they nor we see. Let us take new and fresh steps toward spiritual maturity by being sensitive to and identifying with the struggles of others.

Sweetly may we all agree,
Touched with loving sympathy,
Kindly for each other care;
Every member feel its share.

CHARLES WESLEY

Christian Freedom

*G*od's love is not possessive. While human love tends to be quite possessive, often trying to change or at least improve even the loved one, God lets people be. He leaves them free, even to reject [God]. [God] trusts people not only with creation, but with the work of redemption. Which of us, if [we] were God would trust human beings with the secrets of atomic power? God does.

READINGS IN REDEMPTORIST SPIRITUALITY

When they arrived, they called the church together and related all that God had done with them, and how he had opened a door of faith for the Gentiles.

ACTS 14:27

*O*ur God-given freedom, when considered, is almost terrifying. We are so conscious of our capacity to misuse and abuse our freedom and the freedom of others, that we cannot comprehend a God who would allow us to be free to choose, decide, and act in response to God and in relation to the world around us. But it is in this freedom that we discover our own capacity for maturity: spiritual, psychological, and physical. It is in the positive and creative use of our freedom that we discover who and whose we are.

Long my imprisoned spirit lay,
Fast bound in sin and nature's night;
Thine eye diffused a quickening ray;
I woke, the dungeon framed with light;
My chains fell off, my heart was free,
I rose, went forth, and followed thee.

CHARLES WESLEY

As We Forgive

ometimes we simply do not want to forget the grievances we have toward others. We reinforce and continue to reinfect all of our old wounds.

WILLIAM H. HINSON

For if you forgive others their trespasses, your heavenly Father will also forgive you; but if you do not forgive others, neither will your Father forgive your trespasses.

MATTHEW 6:14-15

*I*t is difficult to let go of the hurts, angers, and bruises that have resulted from the collisions we have had with others. We are fearful that if we forget we will somehow validate what they have done to us. We believe that there is something basically human in saying, "I will forgive, but I will not forget." Yet, every time we pray the Lord's Prayer, we repeat the words, "Forgive us our sins, as we forgive those who sin against us."

The inability to forget causes us to hold on to something that does not contribute to our spiritual or our psychological well-being. We must find ways to forgive, forget, and banish from our inner selves those things that have caused us to be less than whole. Start by really praying the prayer our Savior taught us, rather than just repeating it. Offer up to God those who have wounded you. If we can be forgiven, then surely we can forgive and forget.

Forgive me, Lord, for thy dear Son,
The ill that I this day have done,
That with the world, myself, and thee,
I, ere I sleep, at peace may be.

THOMAS KEN

The Older I Get

In addition to telling me that they want me around a long time, my children also like to cheer me up by saying, "You look good, Dad." Strangely enough, the older I get, the more often I look good; and therefore my handsomeness will reach its peak when they bury me.

BILL COSBY

Children, obey your parents in the Lord, for this is right. "Honor your father and mother"—this is the first commandment with a promise: "so that it may be well with you and you may live long on the earth."

EPHESIANS 6:1-3

The relationship between parents and their adult children is difficult to define. It is fearful and fearsome to acknowledge the aging process that is happening to the parents before their children's eyes. Every compliment that is meant to express a positive word about the maturing process may be viewed with suspicion. Even the words of affirmation are met with a cautious scrutiny. Parents say, "I wonder what they really mean?"

It's best to accept the compliments at face value, without assuming there is a hidden, disparaging message.

I will most gladly spend and be spent for you.
If I love you more, am I to be loved less?

Lost and Found

an you show me the way back to town?" The other man replied, "No, I'm lost too. But we can help each other in this way. We can tell each other which paths we have already tried and been disappointed in. That will help us find the one that leads out."

HAROLD KUSHNER

Jesus said to them, "I am the way, and the truth, and the life. No one comes to the Father except through me."

JOHN 14:6

All of us have known how it feels to be lost, geographically, spiritually, psychologically, or physically. Life is a constant search to find the way out. Harold Kushner, in this little bit of dialogue, reminds us of the commonality of being lost. But, the story tells us, if we share with one another the particularities of our own disappointments, then we can help one another find the way.

Jesus said, "I am the way, the truth, and the life." He is the way—not a signpost—but a pathway to the Father. In the early days of the church, those who followed Jesus were known simply as "followers of the Way." They were on a journey, following Jesus, traveling in his company. The church today should be on this same journey, following Jesus, helping others along the way.

Come, my Way, my Truth, my Life:
Such a way gives us breath,
Such a truth as ends all strife,
Such a life as killeth death.

GEORGE HERBERT

Experiencing the World

*I*n South Central [LA], you don't see the good things about America. But now that I've gone across the United States, I see all the beautiful things. America is a better place than I thought it was. It's a much better place.

Sylvester Monroe

O Lord, how manifold are your works!
In wisdom you have made them all.

Psalm 104:24

No matter where we live—South Central Los Angeles, the South Bronx in New York, or the states of South Carolina or South Dakota—we can so easily miss the wonderful human and environmental diversity of the United States. It is said that travel is "broadening." If our perspective on the nation and the world is limited by what we see and experience in our home community, we miss so much. Experiencing the world beyond can open our eyes to both new beauty and new ugliness.

We may not be able to travel the length and breadth of our land or our world, but we should take every opportunity to read, watch television programs, and talk to others about scenes and events that are beyond the scope of our limited neighborhoods. Where there is beauty, we should rejoice in it; where there is injustice, poverty, or other ugliness, we should take steps to set it right.

Refresh thy people on their toilsome way;
Lead us from night to never-ending day;
Fill all our lives with love and grace divine,
And glory, laud, and praise be ever thine.

DAVID C. ROBERTS

Shalom

*S*halom is much more than personal salvation. It is at once peace, integrity, community, harmony and justice. . . . Shalom is proclaimed. . . . Shalom is lived. . . . Shalom is demonstrated. . . .

J. C. HOEKENDIJK

O LORD, God of my salvation,
when, at night, I cry out in
your presence,
let my prayer come before you;
incline your ear to my cry.

PSALM 88:1-2

*O*ne of my colleagues always signs her letters "Shalom." It is her way of using this ancient word to connect, challenge, and encourage the person receiving her letter. Shalom, for her, is not a word that merely describes the situation that exists, it is her expressed hope, as Hoekendijk wrote, that shalom will be lived.

May our lives become and embody the meaning of shalom.

Grant us thy peace throughout our earthly life;
Peace to thy church from error and from strife;
Peace to our land, the fruit of truth and love;
Peace in each heart, thy Spirit from above.

Thy peace in life, the balm of every pain;
Thy peace in death, the hope to rise again;
Then, when thy voice shall bid our conflict cease,
Call us, O Lord, to thine eternal peace.

JOHN ELLERTON

Person-making

f God's purposes in creation and redemption might be described as the divine art of person-making, then the church is essential to God's whole creative-redemptive process. We become persons and fully human within community. The church represents the beginning of that new humanity that God is calling into being.

RICHARD B. CUNNINGHAM

For no one can lay any foundation other than the one that has been laid; that foundation is Jesus Christ.

1 CORINTHIANS 3:11

Too many churches and too many of us have not yet understood or affirmed the role the church has in helping God perform the art and act of "person-making." It is in community that we experience molding of our lives and bonding with others, and the church must be the community in season and out of season. This process shapes our human journey. God has made us for each other. When we discover the inner person of others, we discover our own humanity.

Elect from every nation,
Yet one o'er all the earth,
Her charter of salvation,
One Lord, one faith, one birth;
One holy name she blesses,
Partakes one holy food,
And to one hope she presses,
With every grace endued.

SAMUEL J. STONE

A Joyful Noise

You can start anywhere—jazz as communication—since it's a circle, and you yourself are the dot in the middle. You, me. . . . Now to wind it all up, with you in the middle—jazz is only what you yourself get out of it.

LANGSTON HUGHES

Make a joyful noise to the LORD, all the earth.

PSALM 100:1

*S*ome of us, not all of us, enjoy jazz. I like its improvisation, creativity, freedom, inclusiveness, and energy. As I listen—for I cannot play an instrument—I am often transported to a state of reflective, meditative, and rhythmic bliss. Jazz, for me, is a reflection of life. Life is pro-active and reactive. Life does not follow a script. Life effects mood changes within me just as jazz does. The physical response that jazz provokes is reflected in my head movements, foot-tapping, and the use of my hands on each other or a convenient piece of furniture to create what I call a "beat." I become what Langston Hughes calls "the dot in the middle."

Take a few moments to reflect on yourself as the dot in the middle of life. Look around the circle around you. Do you enjoy what life is giving you? If not, list some ways you can become pro-active and make changes in your life. It may mean widening your circle.

O lead me Lord, that I may lead
The wandering and the wavering feet;
O feed me, Lord, that I may feed
Thy hungering ones with manna sweet.

FRANCES RIDLEY HAVERGAL

Faithfulness

aithfulness in Christian life does not await full disclosure of all mysteries; instead it awaits our faithfully acting upon what we already know.

NEAL F. FISHER

*Your word is a lamp to my feet
and a light to my path.*

PSALM 119:105

*S*omeone once said to me about the Bible: "I do not worry about the things in the Bible that I do not understand, I worry about the things that I do understand."

My Boston University School of Theology colleague Neal Fisher reminds us that our body of experience and knowledge is sufficient to prompt us into acting out of faith. We spiritually procrastinate by pretending to wait for "disclosure of all mysteries" before we act. In other areas of our lives, we are less fearful of taking leaps of faith. Those of us who have fallen in love have acted on that sensation without comprehending all of its uncertainty and mystery. We often strike out on journeys, move from place to place, take new employment, with some questions still unanswered. Let us be willing to take the same risks in our Christian lives. When you are faced with a spiritual decision, remember to "let go and let God." Move forward in faith.

Help me then in every tribulation
So to trust thy promises, O Lord,
That I lose not faith's sweet consolation
Offered me within thy holy word.
Help me Lord, when toil and trouble meeting,
Ever to take, as from a parent's hand,
One by one, the days, the moments fleeting,
Till I reach the promised land.

DAY BY DAY AND WITH EACH PASSING MOMENT
LINA SANDELL

Our Friends Above

A part of one's immortality is to be remembered. I still remember those who in some way touched my life, who made me laugh or cry, dream and hope. I recall the emptiness and loss I felt when their lives came to an end. Something in me died too, but something of them lived on in me as well.

WOODIE W. WHITE

And there will be no more night; they need no light of lamp or sun, for the Lord God will be their light, and they will reign forever and ever.

REVELATION 22:5

*O*ur lives are the products, the manifestation, the expression of all the other lives that have touched us. Who we are is determined, in part, by our relation and response to those who have touched and influenced us.

One of God's many gifts is the gift of remembrance. Even in the midst of the loneliness that we experience with the loss of a loved one, we can remember that person and our moments together. We therefore are entrusted with both the responsibility and opportunity to embody and express the many ways they have touched us.

One family we dwell in him,
One Church above, beneath,
Though now divided by the stream,
The narrow stream of death;
One army of the living God,
To his command we bow;
Part of his host have crossed the flood,
And part are crossing now.

CHARLES WESLEY

Dreaming

*O*ur dreams must be saddled by the hard facts of our world before we ride them off among the stars. Thus, they become for us the bearers of the new possibility, the enlarged horizon, the great hope.

HOWARD THURMAN

By faith Abraham obeyed when he was called to set out for a place that he was to receive as an inheritance; and he set out, not knowing where he was going.

HEBREWS 11:8

*J*oseph of the Old Testament was a dreamer. Martin Luther King, Jr., electrified a movement and a nation with his "I have a dream" speech. We, too, have dreams. At times they frustrate us and at other times inspire us.

Howard Thurman suggests that we so manage our dreams that they will provide for us, in a world that is suspicious of dreams and dreamers, a vision, a hope, and a platform of encouragement.

Blessed be the name of God
  from age to age,
for wisdom and power are his. . . .
He reveals deep and hidden
  things;
he knows what is in the
  darkness,
and light dwells with him.

DANIEL 2:20, 22

Innocence Found

The next day I took the clothes, my bags, and Guy back to Mother's. I had no idea what I was going to make of my life, but I had given a promise and found my innocence. I swore I'd never lose it again.

Maya Angelou

And when he comes home, he calls together his friends and neighbors, saying to them, "Rejoice with me, for I have found my sheep that was lost."

Luke 15:6

We have the mistaken idea that innocence lost never can be regained. We assume that the mistakes, the violations, and the failures that we have experienced must weigh us down forever. Too many of us allow ourselves to be limited by the negative experiences of our past. We must acknowledge and claim those negatives and then move on.

It is possible to begin again, knowing that we have been shaped and molded by all the experiences of the past. We can allow those experiences to evoke within us a maturity, yes, even a spiritual maturity, that sustains us and may encourage others.

'Tis done: the great transaction's done!
I am my Lord's and he is mine;
He drew me and I followed on,
Charmed to confess the voice divine.

Happy day, happy day,
when Jesus washed my sins away!
He taught me how to watch and pray,
and live rejoicing every day.
Happy day, happy day,
when Jesus washed my sins away!

PHILIP DODDRIDGE

Rubbing Shoulders

I am thankful that I was born to parents who, though not highly educated by today's standards, had a natural feel for the essential music of the English language wedded to an intimate and emotional affection for the great transactions of the Scriptures. Somehow, in the way they thought and spoke, what is African found a cordial meeting with what is Anglo-Saxon.

GARDNER C. TAYLOR

Therefore encourage one another with these words.

1 THESSALONIANS 4:18

We need to seek, on a regular basis, the "cordial meeting" that Gardner Taylor identifies. We have allowed our histories and struggles and assumptions to isolate and insulate us. We have not always valued the interaction that "rubbing shoulders" with people on different journeys and from other cultures can bring.

Some of us still have difficulty accepting, let alone rejoicing, over the grandeur that can emerge when we interact with those who are quite different from us. But whether we admit it or not, each of us is a product of a "meeting" of different experiences and expressions. Praise God for the possibilities our differences offer!

Christ for the world we sing!
The world to Christ we bring,
With joyful song;
The newborn souls, whose days,
Reclaimed from error's ways,
Inspired with hope and praise,
To Christ belong.

SAMUEL WOLCOTT

The World to Christ We Bring

*T*he Wesleyan tradition . . .
began with an evangelical zeal
directed toward the lower classes, the
poor, and the dispossessed. Although its
founder, John Wesley, and his brother
Charles, the poet of Methodism, could
hardly be classified as lower-class, the Methodist Movement
which they started was rooted in a passionate and enthusi-
astic concern for the poorer classes.

WILLIAM B. MCCLAIN

"The poor have good news brought to them."

MATTHEW 11:5

braham Lincoln is quoted as saying, "God must have loved poor people, he made so many of them." Whether Lincoln said this or not, we as persons of faith are challenged to determine whether we unconsciously and consciously avoid, circumvent, and distance ourselves from those whom we label poor.

We are embarrassed by the poor and their poverty. The paradox is that many of us have had and may still have a firsthand acquaintance with what it means to be poor. Yet we separate ourselves from people and communities of poverty.

Whether our history or tradition is Wesleyan or not, our present, if we are to be spiritually whole and wholesome, cannot avoid the fact of poverty and the poor. When we think of the poor, we must be careful not to put them into a category that limits us to a "them" and "us" approach. Rather than hold ourselves apart, we must bring all people into our circle.

Christ for the world we sing!
The world to Christ we bring,
With loving zeal;
The poor and them that mourn,
The faint and overborne,
Sin-sick and sorrow-worn,
Whom Christ doth heal.

SAMUEL WOLCOTT

Roots

It is the roots. Some people doubt it, but I can't do without it. I've had too many good experiences with God to turn around now.

JESSE L. JACKSON

*"Let us go to his dwelling place;
let us worship at his footstool."*

PSALM 132:7

*W*e may think that we are too sophisticated to sing with meaning "Give Me That Old-Time Religion" today. Certainly each generation must discover and claim a spiritual rootedness that speaks to them. Yet, all of us in our spiritual journeys are nurtured by our attachment to the roots of our spiritual past. Our spiritual selves are enriched as we remember and celebrate how God prepared and enriched the soil that nourished our ancestors. We are not detached and autonomous spiritual pilgrims. We are linked to God through those who were linked to God long before we arrived. Their roots are intertwined with ours. Thanks be to God for the connection.

And this is the blessing, wherewith Moses the man of God blessed the children of Israel before his death. And he said, The LORD came from Sinai, and rose up from Seir unto them; he shined forth from mount Paran, and he came with ten thousands of saints. . . . Yea, he loved the people; all his saints are in thy hand: and they sat down at thy feet; every one shall receive of thy words.

DEUTERONOMY 33:1-3 KJV

Melting Stones

*W*e have been motivated by two hopes in writing. . . . First, we believe that people care about injustice and suffering. Second, we hope that once people know the facts, they will act.

An old African proverb says, "Even the hardest stones will melt if boiled long enough." Let's hope . . . to keep the pot boiling.

STACK AND MORTON

At that time I will bring you home,
    at the time when I gather you;
for I will make you renowned and praised
    among all the peoples of the earth,
when I restore your fortunes
    before your eyes, says the LORD.

ZEPHANIAH 3:20

*O*ur rejoicing over the transformation that has taken place in South Africa can obscure the fact that many people of a wide diversity of racial, theological, and political backgrounds worked, wrote, and prayed for change long before the change actually took place.

As Stack and Morton wrote, "People [do] care about injustice" and if we do not grow weary of boiling the stones, change will come. We must never forget those who kept the vision of change alive and vivid. They may not have made the headlines, but they helped make the headlines possible.

I'll praise my Maker while I've breath;
And when my voice is lost in death,
Praise shall employ my nobler powers.
My days of praise shall ne'er be past,
While life, and thought, and being last,
Or immortality endures.

ISAAC WATTS

Celebration

elebration is when we let joy make itself out of our love. Celebration is crazy: the craziness of not submitting even though "they," "the others," the ones who make life impossible seem to have all the power. Celebration is the beginning of confidence, therefore of power.

THOMAS MERTON

O give thanks to the LORD, for
he is good,
for his steadfast love endures
forever.

PSALM 118:29

*S*ome of us have not learned to celebrate. We are so task-oriented or cautious or fearful or guilt-ridden that we are suspicious of celebration and even of those who know how to celebrate. Is it not interesting that Thomas Merton, the cloistered monk, has something of worth to say to those of us outside the cloister about celebration?

What do you have to celebrate today?

> *"Hosanna in the highest!" that ancient*
> *song we sing,*
> *For Christ is our Redeemer, the Lord of*
> *heaven our King.*
> *O may we ever praise him*
> *With heart and life and voice,*
> *And in his blissful presence*
> *Eternally rejoice!*

JEANNETTE THRELFALL

A Just Society

*O*ne might speak of a Christian political ethic, but I refrain from such terminology since it is usually reserved for those who make their ethical systems exclusively dependent on Christian revelation. In a pluralistic society like that of the United States, the need is to affirm an ethic that can be subscribed to by reasonable persons of many faiths or no faith.

DONALD E. MESSER

This blessing has fallen to me,
for I have kept your precepts.

PSALM 119:56

The concern for ethics and ethical behavior transcends categories and loyalties to a religious or political perspective. It is the meeting around what is ethical that allows us to bridge gaps and cross chasms. To suggest that people whose experiences and commitments are different from our own are without ethics is to squander the potential of the creation of community for all of us. We are here to share in the creation of a just and humane society; there are others whose positions and perspectives are different from ours who are ready to share with us.

Long ago the prophet Micah asked the Lord's people, "What doth the LORD require of thee, but to do justly, and to love mercy, and to walk humbly with thy God?" (Micah 6:8 KJV). If we always hold this verse before us, we will act in such a way that a just and humane society will prevail.

> *The voice of God is calling its*
> *summons in our day;*
> *Isaiah heard in Zion, and we now*
> *hear God say:*
> *"Whom shall I send to succor my*
> *people in their need?*
> *Whom shall I send to loosen the*
> *bonds of shame and greed?"*

JOHN HAYNES HOLMES

Success

e cannot and must not stand in judgment of others when it comes to defining success. That was the problem that the women of Wellesley College encountered when they objected to Barbara Bush as their commencement speaker. Success is an extremely personal experience.

MARJORIE L. KIMBROUGH

But Jesus on his part would not entrust himself to them, because he knew all people and needed no one to testify about anyone; for he himself knew what was in everyone.

JOHN 2:24-25

*T*here are times when our political and personal preferences collide, or get mixed up. We would do well to accept definitions from others of their understandings of success, even as we might have political or philosophical differences with them. The joyful mystery of creation is that the Creator has placed in each of us something that can be of value, even an inspiration, to the rest of us.

Let us resist allowing political debate to keep us from affirming personal accomplishment.

Let there be light,
Let there be understanding,
Let all the nations gather,
Let them be face to face.

Open our lips,
Open our minds to ponder,
Open the door of concord
Opening into grace.

FRANCES W. DAVIS

Change

or we are dealing not simply with false notions but with an alienating ethos: a principality and power which shapes not only our thoughts, but our life-styles, self-images, ambitions, commitments, and values.

WALTER WINK

*The LORD has done great things
for us,
and we rejoiced.*

PSALM 126:3

*I*t is trite but very true to say "change is difficult." We have been nurtured and nourished by the traditions and traditional ways of doing. When we are exposed to new truth, we discover that there is something about us that makes us want to cling to the old way. We mistakenly assume that the new understanding and approach invalidates the learnings of the past. That is not so! We are able to move from strength to strength, and maturity to maturity because we have learned well the lessons of the past. Let us be sure that our attachment to "former things" is not our way of stroking our own egos.

For the Spirit of Truth

From the cowardice that dares not face new truth,
from the laziness that is contented with half-truth,
from the arrogance that thinks it knows all truth,
Good Lord, deliver me. Amen.

PRAYER FROM KENYA

Wait on the Lord

A nd so the spirituality of waiting is not simply our waiting for God. It is also participating in God's own waiting for us and in that way coming to share in the deepest love, which is God's love.

HENRI J. M. NOUWEN

Now the LORD came and stood there, calling as before. . . . And Samuel said, "Speak, for your servant is listening."

1 SAMUEL 3:10

*S*uccess, we have convinced ourselves, comes to those who are perpetually busy or appear to be so. The domination of what is called being "task-oriented" affects many of us. We are fearful that if we are not constantly busy, we will fail to achieve or we will fail to impress those whom we think we should impress.

But renewal and revitalization often come when we seek to listen and be guided by the God of our beginnings and endings. Waiting is not a waste of time, it is time well spent.

Speak, Lord, in the stillness,
While I wait on thee;
Hushed my heart to listen
In expectancy.

Fill me with the knowledge
Of thy glorious will;
All thine own good pleasure
In my life fulfill.

E. MAY GRIMES

The Message

rophecy is the voice that God has lent to the silent agony, a voice to the plundered poor, to the profaned riches of the world. It is a form of living, a crossing point of God and man. God is raging in the prophet's words.

ABRAHAM J. HESCHEL

"I am the voice of one crying out in the wilderness, 'Make straight the way of the Lord.' "

JOHN 1:23

It is often difficult for us to understand prophecy or the prophet. We are uncomfortable with the message and, therefore, the messenger. We attribute a certain arrogance to those among us who seem to be so bold and persistent in describing our flaws and our fears. Sometimes we seek to demean and destroy the message by focusing on the flaws of the messenger. We mistakenly believe that if we can bring down the messenger, the message will disappear. But we, individually and collectively, need to be challenged by the messages of the prophets. Those messages have a way of reminding us of things we would prefer to forget.

Then Jeremiah spoke to all the officials and all the people, saying, "It is the LORD who sent me to prophesy against this house and this city all words you have heard. Now therefore amend your ways and your doings, and obey the voice of the LORD your God, and the LORD will change his mind about the disaster that he has pronounced against you. But as for me, here I am in your hands. Do with me as seems good and right to you. Only know for certain that if you put me to death, you will be bringing innocent blood upon yourselves and upon this city and its inhabitants, for in truth the LORD sent me to you to speak all these words in your ears."

JEREMIAH 26:12-15

Human Frailties

e tend to avoid being properly assertive because we are subject to normal human frailties such as irrationality, pride, and fear.

SECRETS OF EXECUTIVE SUCCESS
RODALE PRESS

For he was crucified in weakness, but lives by the power of God. For we are weak in him, but in dealing with you we will live with him by the power of God.

2 CORINTHIANS 13:4

o you think you are subject to normal human frailties? We do not enjoy owning the normalcy of our limitations. Our quest for "super person" status is slowed down when we admit to limitations. But how liberating it is to remember that we do possess limitations, and that they are normal.

The first step to take when wishing to overcome these human frailties is to pray for strength. A line from "Just a Closer Walk with Thee" can serve as a reminder that, with the help of our blessed Savior, normal human frailties can become a source of strength: "I am weak, but thou art strong . . ."

I am weak but thou art strong!
Jesus, keep me from all wrong:
I'll be satisfied as long
As I walk, let me walk close to thee.

Through this world of toil and snares,
If I falter, Lord, who cares?
Who with me my burden shares?
None but thee, dear Lord, none but thee.

AUTHOR UNKNOWN

Write Me a Letter

've found that even though we do make phone calls, a letter has value. It's possible to tell a story in a more coherent way in a letter. I'm less likely to forget matters I want to tell about. And the recipients have material evidence that they can save and re-read and so prolong and deepen the otherwise transient moment of relationship.

Grace to you and peace from God our Father and the Lord Jesus Christ.

ROMANS 1:7*b*

My mother used to write each of her four children once a week. During the years she lived with us, she would hand deliver her letter to Grace and me. It was her way of providing "material evidence" of our relationship.

Think of the letters Paul and the other apostles wrote to the early church. Those letters were so important that they were passed around, copied, read and re-read, and finally became part of the body of scripture we read today. Our words may not carry the weight of the apostles', but the letters we write have value both in the moments that they are first read and in times long after. Conversations and phone calls have their place, but letters live long after these other communications have been forgotten.

Paul, an apostle of Christ Jesus by the will of God, for the sake of the promise of life that is in Christ Jesus, to Timothy, my beloved child: . . .

I am grateful to God . . . when I remember you constantly in my prayers night and day. . . . I am reminded of your sincere faith, a faith that lived first in your grandmother Lois and your mother Eunice and now, I am sure, lives in you.

2 TIMOTHY 1:1-3, 5

The Spirit Says Come

here is another reason why some of us shy away from the Spirit. Many fear being grasped by an invisible presence we cannot control. In this regard, we share the problematics of spiritual experience throughout all ages.

JAMES FORBES

When the day of Pentecost had come, they were all together in one place. And suddenly from heaven there came a sound like the rush of a violent wind, and it filled the entire house where they were sitting. Divided tongues, as of fire, appeared among them, and a tongue rested on each of them. All of them were filled with the Holy Spirit and began to speak in other languages, as the Spirit gave them ability.

ACTS 2:1-4

*J*ohn Wesley talked about an experience that left his "heart strangely warmed." Others of us can and do identify experiences that have put us in touch with the Holy Spirit in such a powerful way that we were transformed. However, there are those persons who are resistant to Spirit experiences.

Opening ourselves to the power of the Holy Spirit can be a frightening thing. But, if we are willing to risk the encounter, we may find that the working of the Spirit can do to us and for us all that we have been seeking in other ways and places.

O Great Spirit,
  whose breath gives life to the world,
  and whose voice is heard in the soft breeze:
We need your strength and wisdom.
Cause us to walk in beauty. Give us eyes
  ever to behold the red and purple sunset.
Make us wise so that we may understand
  what you have taught us.
Help us learn the lessons you have hidden
  in every leaf and rock.
Make us always ready to come to you
  with clean hands and steady eyes,
so when life fades, like the fading sunset,
  our spirits may come to you without shame.
        Amen.

TRADITIONAL NATIVE AMERICAN PRAYER

Your First Works

*I*n the church I come from we were counseled from time to time to do our first works over. To do your first works over means to reexamine everything. Go back to where you started, or as far back as you can, examine all of it, travel your road again, and tell the truth about it. Sing or shout or testify or keep it to yourself, but know whence you came.

JAMES BALDWIN

Therefore let the entire house of Israel know with certainty that God has made him both Lord and Messiah, this Jesus whom you crucified.

ACTS 2:36

*S*eldom do we give much time to going back to where we started. We unconsciously believe that there is no turning back. James Baldwin reminds all of us of an eternal truth: our journey into the future can be helpfully shaped as we remember where we have been.

What we do with those rediscoveries is up to us. It may not be helpful to hold on too long to those early beginning places, but it is never helpful to fail to remember and revisit those places from whence we came. Your darkest day may lighten up in a later time when you can look back on it from a distance filled with new learnings and knowledge.

The steadfast love of the LORD never ceases,
his mercies never come to an end;
they are new every morning;
great is your faithfulness.

LAMENTATIONS 3:22-23

A Positive Approach

ut because of this the mosquito has a guilty conscience. To this day she goes about whining in people's ears. "ZEEE! Is everyone still angry with me?" When she does that she gets an honest answer. K-P O W!

VERNA AARADEMA
A WEST AFRICAN TALE

If I speak in the tongues of mortals and of angels, but do not have love, I am a noisy gong or a clanging cymbal.

1 CORINTHIANS 13:1

This children's story from West Africa vividly describes the havoc brought about by the mosquito's buzzing in the ear of an iguana. The response of the iguana initiates a chain reaction that negatively affects a number of the animals in the jungle.

When a mosquito buzzes around us, we try to destroy the source. In fact, we are prone to handle any annoyance with an effort to destroy the source. Perhaps a better way might be to put on a repellent that keeps the mosquito away. Carrying the thought a step further, perhaps we should put on an attitude, a perspective, a positive approach, that will keep other annoyances at bay. We can draw closer to God, turning the annoyance over to God, resting in the promise that God does care for us.

Whenever I am tempted,
Whenever clouds arise,
When songs give place to sighing,
When hope within me dies,
I draw the closer to him,
From care he sets me free;
His eye is on the sparrow,
And I know he watches me.

HIS EYE IS ON THE SPARROW
CIVILLA D. MARTIN

Let's Go

eter Drucker has identified three major risks in innovation. The first is that it will make obsolete current practices and patterns of operation. The second is that it will fail. The third is that it will succeed—but in succeeding it may produce unforeseen consequences that create new problems.

LYLE E. SCHALLER

But when God, who had set me apart before I was born and called me through his grace, was pleased to reveal his Son to me, so that I might proclaim him among the Gentiles, I did not confer with any human being, nor did I go up to Jerusalem to those who were already apostles before me, but I went away at once into Arabia, and afterwards I returned to Damascus.

GALATIANS 1:15-17

*I*nnovation, change, transformation, or whatever word we want to use, is easier spoken than accomplished. We all wish that we could change *without* changing. We would rather just avoid the trauma caused by something new.

Despite our resistance, every day is a day of change. We change without knowing it. Some of us work hard to ignore it, as if by doing so we can keep it from happening. Yet to resist change is to miss out on growing. Suppose the Hebrews had given in to their fears and had never begun the journey to the Promised Land? Suppose our Freedom Fighters had ignored injustice rather than fought against it? Suppose everyone in the medical community had kept on treating illnesses as they did in the nineteenth century?

When you are facing a change in your life, don't ignore it—embrace it. What joy comes to us when we are able to look change in the face and say, "Let's go!"

O come and dwell in me,
Spirit of power within,
And bring the glorious
    liberty
From sorrow, fear, and sin.

CHARLES WESLEY

107

I Believe

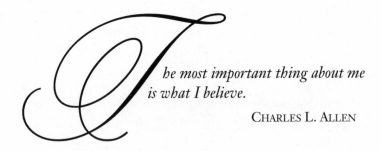 *he most important thing about me is what I believe.*

CHARLES L. ALLEN

"Do not let your hearts be troubled. Believe in God, believe also in me."

JOHN 14:1

Résumés, biographical sketches, and introductions before speeches and sermons may describe what a person has accomplished, but they seldom capture what he or she believes.

We are what we believe. Our lives are shaped by the core of our belief system. The things we do, the things we refrain from doing, the opinions we have, the stands we take, all reflect what it is we believe.

As Christians our belief is grounded on Jesus Christ. If we truly believe in and follow him, our daily lives will be a reflection of Christ.

We would see Jesus, Mary's son most holy,
Light of the village life from day to day;
Shining revealed through every task most lowly,
The Christ of God, the life, the truth, the way.

J. EDGAR PARK

Peace

When we live in peace, our lives are not tormented by the anguish of stress.

BELL HOOKS

"Glory to God in the highest heaven, and on earth peace among those whom he favors!"

LUKE 2:14

*P*eace, we know, is more than the absence of war. It is an attitude, a practice, a way of life. Those among us who have decided not to allow the stresses of life to destroy their peace have discovered a secret that enriches their lives.

We can get sucked into arguments that evoke anguish within us and others and discover that we have allowed ourselves to be shaped—or perhaps mis-shaped—by factors outside ourselves.

Blessed are they who have determined that a life and spirit of peace will be their signature. We can all obtain that peace by turning our lives over to the Prince of Peace.

Be still, my soul: your God will undertake
To guide the future, as in ages past.
Your hope, your confidence let nothing shake;
All now mysterious shall be bright at last.
Be still, my soul: the waves and winds still know
The Christ who ruled them while he dwelt below.

KATHARINA VON SCHLEGEL

"Like a Baby"

*he children were nestled all
snug in their beds,
while visions of sugar plums danced
in their heads.*

CLEMENT C. MOORE

"*Therefore I tell you, do not worry about your life, what you will eat or what you will drink, or about your body, what you will wear. Is not life more than food, and the body more than clothing? Look at the birds of the air; they neither sow nor reap nor gather into barns, and yet your heavenly Father feeds them. Are you not of more value than they?*"

MATTHEW 6:25-26

112

*C*hildren have the capacity to make their sleep a time of renewal and visioning. We adults describe our rare experiences of restful sleep by saying, "I slept like a baby."

It may be that the way we begin to "become like little children" is to imitate their sleeping habits. Then we may have dreams and visions that make our waking moments joyful and rewarding.

The first step in making going to bed a restful and renewing experience is to cast all our cares on God. Be sure part of your nighttime ritual includes thanking God for the day and asking God to be with you through the night. Do not let the nighttime become a time for dwelling on problems, real or imagined. Give those feelings over to God. God cares for you.

Be still, my soul: the Lord is on your side.
Bear patiently the cross of grief or pain;
Leave to your God to order and provide;
In every change God faithful will remain.
Be still, my soul: your best, your heavenly friend,
Through thorny ways leads to a joyful end.

KATHARINA VON SCHLEGEL

Personality

esus didn't say we have to love the personality of everyone we know. Just love the child within him or her.

MARILYN MORGAN HELLEBERG

"You have heard that it was said, 'You shall love your neighbor and hate your enemy.' But I say to you, Love your enemies and pray for those who persecute you."

MATTHEW 5:43-44

*M*s. Helleberg is speaking of a neighbor she found absolutely obnoxious. After one particularly annoying incident she mentioned her frustration to a trusted spiritual advisor. His answer—"Jesus didn't say we have to love the personality of everyone we know. *Just love the child of God within her*"—was incredibly freeing. Somehow, just admitting that she didn't care for this woman took the edge off the neighbor's frustrating personality. Once the edge was gone, Ms. Helleberg found she was able to ask God for help in seeing the child of God within her neighbor.

Most days we will meet someone who "rubs us the wrong way." When that happens, acknowledge in your heart that for some unknown reason, that person is just not on your wavelength. Then thank God for that person and for creating humanity in such a diversity of personality.

*Take thou our hearts, O Christ—they are
        thine own;
Come thou within our soul and claim thy
        throne,
Help us to shed abroad thy generous love;
Use us to make the earth like heaven above.*

WILLIAM HIRAM FOULKES

Spiritual Wholeness

Our justice concerns will emerge not from the outside, . . . but from within as we identify more and more with Jesus, our model for spiritual wholeness. From the gift of his call to share his ministry will arise our desire and the recognition of our duty to live a life of justice. The gift of Christ's presence will enable us to carry out the call.

MENNONITE MUTUAL AID

Again I saw all the oppressions that are practiced under the sun. Look, the tears of the oppressed—with no one to comfort them! On the side of their oppressors there was power.

ECCLESIASTES 4:1

God calls us to do justice! Most of us can quote Micah 6:8: "[God] has told you, O mortal, what is good; and what does the LORD require of you but to do justice, and to love kindness, and to walk humbly with your God?" Other Old Testament prophets also spoke of the importance of God's people following the way of justice. "Let justice roll down like waters, and righteousness like an everflowing stream" (Amos 5:24).

But justice concerns are not just Old Testament concerns. We who follow the way of Christ must also follow the way of justice. Jesus himself is our model. He calls us to do justice in our own day-to-day world. His call is clear: we are to feed the hungry, give the thirsty water, aid the stranger, comfort the sick, visit those in prison. Let us never ask, "Lord, when did we see you . . . ?" We have only to open our eyes. Justice is a Christian concern.

Come, divine Interpreter,
bring me eyes thy book to read,
ears the mystic words to hear,
words which did from thee proceed,
words that endless bliss impart,
kept in an obedient heart.

All who read, or hear, are blessed,
if thy plain commands we do;
of thy kingdom here possessed,
thee we shall in glory view
when thou comest on earth to abide,
reign triumphant at thy side.

CHARLES WESLEY

Teachers

Invest in the human soul. Who knows, it might be a diamond in the rough.

MARY MCLEOD BETHUNE

"Go therefore and make disciples of all nations, baptizing them in the name of the Father and of the Son and of the Holy Spirit, and teaching them to obey everything that I have commanded you. And remember, I am with you always, to the end of the age."

MATTHEW 28:19-20

The first memorial to an African American and a woman in Washington D.C.'s public parks honors the late Dr. Mary McLeod Bethune, educator, humanitarian, and churchwoman. A sculpture of Dr. Bethune and two African American children is located in Lincoln Park in line with the Emancipation Group, featuring Abraham Lincoln and a freed slave. Dr. Bethune left America a rich legacy. Part of her classic "Last Will and Testament" reads, "I leave you love, hope, faith. I leave you racial dignity. I leave you a thirst for education."

Most of us can recall a teacher who encouraged us, who helped us overcome some stumbling block, who opened for us the windows of knowledge and learning. Beautiful stories have appeared in newspapers from time to time telling of children, largely written off by society, who went on to become highly successful, productive citizens because a teacher cared.

Can you invest in a human soul?

I sit down alone, only God is here;
In his presence I open, I read his books;
And what I thus learn, I teach.

JOHN WESLEY

Called Back to the Fire

*D*eep in the forest a call was sounding, and as often as he heard this call, mysteriously thrilling and luring, he felt compelled to turn his back upon the fire and the beaten earth around it, and plunge into the forest, and on and on, he knew not where or why; nor did he wonder where or why, the call sounding imperiously deep in the forest. But as often as he gained the soft unbroken earth and the green shade, the love of John Thornton brought him back to the fire again.

JACK LONDON

Yet all these, though they were commended for their faith, did not receive what was promised, since God had provided something better so that they would not, apart from us, be made perfect.

HEBREWS 11:39-40

*I*n his book *Trails and Turnpikes*, Carl E. Price likens us to the wolf in Jack London's tale, *The Call of the Wild*. We are often tempted to give up the fight for human rights, for justice in government, for honesty in business, for integrity in our relationships, for all the specific ways we seek to do good. We might say that even when we are trying to do our best, our baser nature keeps luring us away from the campfire, away from the love of God.

When we struggle, we need to remember the examples of those who have gone before us, not just prophets and apostles, but our own dear friends and kin who loved us and taught us by example to do the right thing. By remembering those examples, Price says, "We are called back to the fire." Spiritual health does not come automatically; we have to work at it. Struggle in itself is not defeating; giving in to the struggle, to our baser nature, is.

We turn to the word of God for help, we turn to human examples, we turn to the example of our blessed Lord. Help is there. We need only to stir up the dying embers.

This little light of mine,
I'm goin'-a let it shine,
This little light of mine,
I'm goin'-a let it shine,
This little light of mine,
I'm goin'-a let it shine,
let it shine, let it shine,
let it shine.

AFRICAN AMERICAN SPIRITUAL

Expectations

o one rises to low expectations.

LES BROWN

*Finally, beloved, whatever is true, whatever is honorable,
whatever is just, whatever is pure, whatever is pleasing,
whatever is commendable, if there is any excellence and if
there is anything worthy of praise, think about these
things.*

PHILIPPIANS 4:8

How many times do we say or think, "I'm doing the best I can"? How many times when we say those words are we really doing the best we can? Most of the time that phrase is uttered as an excuse when we really are not trying to do, let alone doing, anywhere near our best. Often our failures spring not from our actions, but from our inactions. Madeleine L'Engle in *A Circle of Quiet* repeats a Jewish legend which says that when Moses first struck the waters of the Red Sea with his staff nothing happened. Only when one of the Israelite men stuck his foot into the water did the sea part. Only a legend, but what a story is there. *"No one rises to low expectations!"*

Christ has no body now on earth but yours, no hands but yours, no feet but yours; yours are the eyes through which to look at Christ's compassion to the world, yours are the feet with which he is to go about doing good, and yours are the hands with which he is to bless us now.

TERESA OF AVILA

God's Will

A s surely as the unfolding rose is in the planted seed, God's will is planted within you. It is an active, living thing, waiting only for your recognition. . . . Trust God's will to unfold from within you, and his best will surely come to you.

MARILYN MORGAN HELLEBERG

"Father, I desire that those also, whom you have given me, may be with me where I am, to see my glory, which you have given me because you loved me before the foundation of the world."

JOHN 17:24

How often we wonder about God's will for our lives. Perhaps the trouble is that we never really try to discern God's will. We run around saying, "What would you have me do, Lord?" but we don't really expect God to answer. I recently heard a Sunday school teacher say that many of our prayers are answered, but since we do not like the answer we get, we keep on praying as if God has not heard.

Maybe what we need to do is *decrease the number of times we pray* to know God's will, and *increase the amount of time we spend listening* for an answer. God's will is planted within us—we need to allow it to grow.

Do not give up.... When you first begin, you find only darkness and as it were a cloud of unknowing. You don't know what this means except that in your will you feel a simple, steadfast intention reaching out towards God.... Reconcile yourself to wait in this darkness as long as is necessary, but still go on longing after him whom you love.

FROM *THE CLOUD OF UNKNOWING*
(FOURTEENTH CENTURY)

A Paradox

We are not valuable because of any contribution we make. We are objects of God's love simply because we are God's own. God loves us even when the investment of love brings no return.

ROBERT A. WALLACE

"Are not five sparrows sold for two pennies? Yet not one of them is forgotten in God's sight. But even the hairs of your head are all counted. Do not be afraid; you are of more value than many sparrows."

LUKE 12:6-7

This affirmation of God's love for us appears again and again in the Bible. God loves us no matter what. It is very much like, but even more than, the love of a parent for a child. As parents we may despair that our children do not always behave as we would wish, but certainly we'd not give them up or give up on them. We would not exchange the life of one to save the life of another.

Yet that is just what God did, giving the life of an only son so that we might live. We don't have to do a thing to earn that love. But here is the paradox: the more we realize that we don't have to earn God's love, the more we want to share that love with others. And that sharing takes the form of doing. The realization that we are unconditionally loved is what motivates us to feed the hungry, give aid and comfort to the stranger, visit those who are sick or in prison, struggle for justice for all God's children.

Give me, good Lord, a full faith, a firm hope and a fervent charity, a love to thee incomparable above the love to myself.

Give me, good Lord, a longing to be with thee, not for the avoiding of the calamities of this world, nor so much for the attaining of the joys of heaven, as for the love of thee.

THOMAS MORE

Stress

It is no wonder more people don't really know God today if being still and quiet is the way to do so.

CAROLE CUPPLES

And he said, Go forth and stand upon the mount before the LORD. And, behold, the LORD passed by, and a great and strong wind rent the mountains, and brake in pieces the rocks before the LORD; but the LORD was not in the wind: and after the wind an earthquake; but the LORD was not in the earthquake: And after the earthquake a fire; but the LORD was not in the fire: and after the fire a still small voice.

1 KINGS 19:11-12 KJV

We live in a time when no one recognizes the benefits of the "lazy, hazy, crazy days of summer." We feel we have to be engaged in some sort of activity even when we are not working. Children no longer shuffle through vacation periods in aimless, unstructured playing, but instead are driven around to various prescribed activities—dance, karate, baseball, and on and on. Adults once worked from sunup to sundown (often with a little breather in the hottest part of the day). Now we plug in and interface far into the night hours.

No wonder we sometimes feel God is silent. The still small voice cannot be heard over the clamoring of human activity. We do not have time to listen and we do not hear. Not only do we fail to hear the voice of God, we fail to hear the voices of our families, our friends, and those in the world who need our help as the people of God. There is no need to enter a cloister or monastery, but we have a great need to carve out time for ourselves to pray, to read God's word, and to listen quietly for God's voice. Once we've allowed that to happen, we will begin to hear the other voices as well.

O Lord, the Scripture says "there is a time for silence and a time for speech." Savior, teach me the silence of humility, the silence of wisdom, the silence of love, the silence of perfection, the silence that speaks without words, the silence of faith.

FRANKFURT PRAYER
(SIXTEENTH CENTURY)

As Ourselves?

*T*o allow the hungry [person] to remain hungry would be blasphemy against God and one's neighbor, for what is nearest to God is precisely the need of one's neighbor. . . . To provide the hungry [person] with bread is to prepare the way for the coming of grace.

DIETRICH BONHOEFFER

"You shall love the Lord your God with all your heart, and with all your soul, and with all your strength, and with all your mind; and your neighbor as yourself."

LUKE 10:27

*S*o often, like the lawyer in the parable of the good Samaritan, we try to justify ourselves. We give to charities—at least to those serving people of whom we, in some way, approve. We go to church—at least most of the time. But it seems that part of our justification has become focused on the last word of that verse—*yourself*. Charity, we say, begins at home. We want everything we feel we are entitled to, we want our children to have everything their friends have, and if that means turning away from the homeless person on the street, the person with AIDS, the children forced to work in sweat shops, then that's just the way it has to be. When the house is paid for, when the children finish college, when we're sure we have plenty saved up for our old age, then we'll see about increasing our charitable gifts.

Bonhoeffer is very clear: this attitude is blasphemy against God and one's neighbor. The writer of First John had no doubts either. "How does God's love abide in anyone who has the world's goods and sees a brother or sister in need and yet refuses help?" (1 John 3:17) So if we are first loving God, then the best way to live out that love is to share what we have with our neighbor. Surely this is the means to grace.

Little children, let us love, not in word or speech, but in truth and action. . . . And this is his commandment, that we should believe in the name of his Son Jesus Christ and love one another, just as he has commanded us. All who obey his commandments abide in him and he abides in them. And by this we know that he abides in us, by the Spirit that he has given us.
1 JOHN 3:18, 23-24

Indexes

INDEX OF SCRIPTURE

Indexes

INDEX OF SUBJECTS

INDEX OF SOURCES

Indexes